What's on the Menu?
All of Me!

Literary Entrees
Prepared By

Walee

iUniverse, Inc.

New York Lincoln Shanghai

What's on the Menu? All of Me!
Literary Entrees Prepared By Walee

iUniverse books may be ordered through booksellers or by contacting:

iUniverse
2021 Pine Lake Road, Suite 100
Lincoln, NE 68512
www.iuniverse.com
1-800-Authors (1-800-288-4677)

ISBN-13: 978-0-595-39041-0 (pbk)
ISBN-13: 978-0-595-83431-0 (ebk)
ISBN-10: 0-595-39041-2 (pbk)
ISBN-10: 0-595-83431-0 (ebk)

Printed in the United States of America

Contents

Acknowledgements

Shout outs to the following:

To all people who supported **Confession is Good for the Soul: Lyrics of Love, Lullabies of Pain**. It was with you in mind that this second collection was conceived.

To the greatest Management Team, **Whittle and Williams**: I love, trust, appreciate and respect you so very much.

To the world's wackiest family members: **The Jacksons, The Johnsons, The Tolivers, The Jeters** and **The Armours**. We've accomplished so much and there's still so much more left to do.

Cheryl: Even though you are the Queen of Baby Mama Drama, you're still the perfect melody in my rhyme.

To my son, Wesley: I don't always have the answers you want to hear, but I'll always have the love that you need.

Robert C. Morton: Who says an ole dog can't learn new tricks? 194??? Yeah, right!

Karla, Jane, Darlene, Micah, Kim, Angel, Lillian, Daniel and Angela: You've come into my life at the right time. Here's to an enduring friendship!

Cydnie, Shanda and Alonzo: Thanks for making my first experience the best!!!

Colleen, Suzanne, Sandy, Carrie, MaryAnn, Mary and Amar: You listen so well! Thanks for your personal and professional support.

Delpera: you give the best hugs!

OHS in da House!: Veronica, Robin, Fatimah, Judy, Jon-Jon: Just because you're you!

Dion Johnson and the rest of the Weekend Jam Squad (Vikki, Betty, Janice, Vicky, Barry, Rob, Dan, Jerry, Shirley, Charmelle, Jill, Monica, Darel, Delores, Sheila, Janice, Gloria, Luandra, Devon, Alicia, et al): Thanks for helping me get into great conditioning shape not just for the book tour but for life in general.

Philip and Carolyn McRimmon: Where do I begin??? There are not enough days and ways to express the depth of my affection for you both.

Bobbie; Cameron; Dennis, Janice; Kennard; Philip; Rob; Stacey: My favorite "Moon People!"

Cynthia, Nikki, Renee, Tracey, Karen, Alisha, Michael, Avon, Deborah…and you too, Mr. No Show Marcus: OK, whose turn is it to host the next jam?

Dr. Allgood, Dr. Forbes, Dr. McPherson, and Dr. Powell: While I'm continually astounded by your academic and medical accomplishments, I'm more impressed with your humanity.

John & Stacey: And this too shall pass.

Kiesha: It is not the days, weeks or months that matter as we just pick up from where we left off and it is still ALL GOOD! Your red pen is the sword that cuts deep. Your smile is the bandage that makes it all better.

Maceo: Thank you for introducing me to Flora Purim and…

Rajabu: What happens at the Fraternity Meetings stays at the Fraternity Meetings.

Indy West: When are you fixing me breakfast, woman?

My Security Council (or is that Security Blanket???):

Walter J.—for ensuring that his seed that created me wasn't sprayed or swallowed

Abdul M.—for recognizing the child in me that needed the father in you

Lamont P.—for not forwarding an invoice for your words of guidance, wisdom and support

Eddie G.—for inspiring me to want to be like you when I finally decide to grow up

Earl J.—for taking me from the Brown Betty to the White Girl to the Green Hornet to the Golden Lady

When I was a child, I spoke as a child, I understood as a child, I thought as a child: but when I became a man, I put away childish things.

1 Corinthians 13:11

Chapter 1

The Appetizers

I am a weapon of mass seduction
with a willingness to give an oral instruction
a future candidate for a Hall of Fame induction
without further adieu, allow me the introduction

Will

Always

LoveU

Everyday

Eternally

A Miranda Warning
Who knew that a tongue could be charged with "assault with a deadly weapon?"

What's On the Menu?
Allow me to reintroduce myself…Be afraid…Be very afraid…

Mmm, mmm good!
Taste me, and smack your lips in content.

Tonight's the night for…
Seizing opportunities and mastering the possibilities.

A Tisket, a Tasket, I Want to Eat What's in Your Basket!
  A tongue darts and dangles, while a throat chokes and strangles.

I Just Want To Thank You
  My heartbeat is heartfelt for you.

Happy Anniversary, Baby
  And another one, and another one, and another one...

A Seminar in Maximizing Your Orgasm
  Bring an apple for the teacher and you'll get an "A."

I'm going to wear you out!
  When it's all said and done, baby, you are indeed the one.

A Miranda Warning

You have the right to remain silent
but it will be nearly impossible for you to do so.
You are hereby forewarned that this tongue is on the FBI's Most Wanted
List.
Not for what it can say, but what it is capable of making you do
against your will,
against your wishes,
even against your religion.
Everything you say can and will be used to further escalate my arousal.
You have the right to speak to an attorney
and to have one present during my oral consumption of you.
I am not opposed to a ménage a trois,
but I don't think you want anyone on this planet to see the way your face
will be contorted,
your speech rendered unintelligible,
nor your legs twisted in three-dimensional angles that have yet to be cal-
culated by mathematicians.
You think I'm playing? I'm not conceited, I'm convinced!!!
This tongue is under surveillance with global mad scientists plotting to
capture it,
cut it out,
lock it up,
study it,
attempt to clone it,
mass produce it,
and become trillionaires once they have harnessed its awesome power.
This is your last time to get dressed, walk out that door and we shall
never speak of this moment again.
You're still here?
You say you are not going anywhere?
OK, but remember,
I warned you.

What's on the menu?

Good evening.
My name is Walee
and I'll be your attendant this evening.
Is this your first time at MyDickTastesSoGood?
Welcome!
Allow me to share tonight's specials with you.
We have several especially prepared appetizers beginning with
Butterfly Eyelash Kisses,
Sensuous Snacking On Skin
and
Lavish Licks Of Labia.

The soupe de jour is Gumbo YaYa.
"YaYa" gets its name from the French expression of a mistake,
since the Chef thinks he has burnt the roux (but not). The trick is a very
dark
brown chocolate colored roux that is rich in flavor. The gumbo is made
with a slow simmered turkey stock, andouille sausage, and pulled turkey
meat.[1]

Our main course specials include
Beef tenderloin fillets wrapped in puff pastry with a creamy sauce
Roast Turkey, Caramelized Onion and Saga Blue Cheese on Grilled
Sourdough
Rack of Lamb with Lavender Honey
and
Porterhouse Steak with Hoisin Barbecue Sauce and Rosemary and Garlic
Fingerling

---

[1]   Chef Emile L. Stieffel, Aurora Catering, Inc.

You need additional information?
Simply put, we offer the Finest in Fulsome Fits of Fucking!
We can have
your kittykat kissed and caressed,
your salmon sautéed and stroked,
your punani pleasured and prayed to

Do we have take out?
Ma'am, this is an established, award winning five-diamond restaurant!
HOWEVER, as it is our aim to please all who enter, we will
TAKE you out,
TURN you out,
TOSS you over,
TEASE you tenderly,
TWIST you gingerly, and
TUCK you in

A doggie bag? How about doggie style!

And for dessert we can amorously offer
mangotippednipplestobesuckledbyme
and
astrawberrycoveredcholocatedicktobesuckedbyyou

Pardon me; I neglected to mention our wine list. We have an extensive offering to complement your meal. The open bar is always top shelf, offering premium brand service of Cocktails and Highballs. I highly recommend the Penile Grigio. Should you need a more enhanced thirst quencher, our house special protein shake, The Penis Colada, should do just the trick. It takes a while to prepare and ultimately deliver, but it is THE favorite of a few of our select patrons. A special scented napkin comes with it to wipe away any remaining drops that may find itself on your lips, cheek, forehead, ear, hair…

Oh, I see that you've noticed the **WWW Special**.
It is discriminately offered to our most valued clients.
What is it? Quite frankly, it is me.
ALL of me.
ALL that you can nibble,
ALL that you can lick,
ALL that you can take in,
ALL that you can choke on,
ALL that you can swallow.
It is the joie de vivre
It is the raison d'etre
It is simply the most intense orgasm you will ever experience!

Antartic chills will soar throughout your body
Leaving you quivering, shivering and asking for deliverance
Longing to never be released from this feeling, this moment, and this
instant.

Over and over you will plead for mercy as the
Fulfillment of you is my only goal and objective

Merci, beaucoup…mi amore es solamente para ti
Earth shattering, eruption splattering leading to operatic scatting

Yodel-Ay, Yodel-Ay-Ee-Oooh!!!

Let me give you a few moments to consider your options. Just ring this bell, and I will return to take your order. Again, welcome to the **Wonderful World of Walee**.

Mmm, mmm good!

you can beat my master drum to erection
while I eat your sugar plum to perfection

I can work my tongue to a mambo beat
in places you never thought were meant to eat

I can have you coming faster than the Falls of Niagra
and I don't need any assistance from a blue pill named Viagra

so there is no use in denying the intensity of my gaze
      nor the simmer of my touch
and there is no use in delaying the gratification
      that you desire and deserve so very much
and there is no use in denying you the taste
      of this double dipped scoop of chocolate deluxe
and there is no use in delaying the spasms
      caused by multiple orgasms resulting in a luminous flux

the Borg said it best,
"Resistance is futile!"

so give in to your temptation
taste me, and smack your lips in content
don't try to act shy now
I'm not R. Kelly, and you are way past the age of consent

you didn't know it could be so edible, huh?
you didn't know it could be so incredible, huh?

allow me to feast upon your cupcakes
deliciously decadent

now on to your devils food cake
hotter than a jalapeno and sweeter than a cappuccino

you didn't know it could be so edible, huh?
you didn't know it could be so incredible, huh?

let us depart from the doorway as we continue the foreplay
lured by the arrival of a creamy, sweet frosting just begging for the tasting
providing all the right nutrients and ingredients
to create life
and if applied properly, clear acne

you didn't know it could be so edible, huh?
you didn't know it could be so incredible, huh?

this dick is so delickous so come get sum, like dim sum and then some more
and for an encore, I'll participate and reciprocate and anticipate your
punani salivate

you didn't know it could be so edible, huh?
you didn't know it could be so incredible, huh?

oh, what a tantalizing treat
and oh, what a succulent feast
licking, nibbling, biting, swirling, savoring, swallowing

you just didn't know it could be so edible, huh?
you just didn't know it could be so incredible, huh?

Mmm, mmm, good!

Tonight's the night for...

subtle stares
knowing what's what
an obvious glare
catches eyes wide shut

teeth are being licked
legs are being uncrossed
somebody's getting dicked
and a salad will be tossed

a dance to the pendulum beat
tensions about to be released
an unraveling of the conundrum heat
and sexual indiscretions will not be policed

a slip of the tongue
a slip of the lips
a tug at the hung
a tug at the hips

the thrill of the anticipation
heritage from Mesopotamia
the anxiety of an oral accommodation
hoping the nut tastes like Macadamia

a tender twist of the mustachio
a gentle caress of a swollen breast
a bathroom nibble on the pistachio
a whole lot of swallowing of what comes next

puffs and pants
and huffs and chants
an explosive jet stream arrives

gargling and choking
and pressure releasing stroking
knock, knock, knock…oops, here comes a surprise

a patron enters as we readjust our clothes
and gives us a disapproving look
I pick out my fro as she powders her nose
we confirm tomorrow in our appointment book

Tonight's the night for…

A Tisket, A Tasket, I Want To Eat What's In Your Basket

A quarter of the circumference of a circle…this defines a right angle

so come over here and take your rightful place
and grace your throne upon my face
let your lava flow while leaving a trace
inside your panties, hot silk and cool lace

YOU control the rhythm
YOU control the rhyme
YOU define the algorithm
so please, rewind your grind

sniffing your panties as if they were a nice Chianti
punani juices tasting like rum punch
so pose for the snapshot as I eat out your backshot
I lap it up and sap it up like its Captain Crunch

my teeth are now entangled in your Victoria Secret
my tongue darts and dangles inside your clitoria secret
my throat closes and strangles from your Eva Longoria secret
my face becomes all mangled as you release your euphoria secret

and now the finale to this secret rendevous
is swallowing the lilies of your valley after our rende-screw
and until we meet again I bid you adieu
but first and foremost let me say thank you

for keeping it clean and keeping it tight
for making me scream and making me bite
for…
producing tears and

reducing fears and
inducing cheers and
seducing my ears
with your chanting and panting and ranting, oh my
with your gnashing and splashing and thrashing, oh my
with your cravings and ravings and leg wavings, oh my
with your bouncing and pouncing and announcing
OH MY GOD, I'M CUUUUUMMMMMIIIIIINNNNGGGG!!!!

I Just Want To Thank You

I just want to thank you
for holding me the way that I need to be held
for kissing me the way that I need be to kissed
and for loving me the way that I need to be loved

you found me so profoundly at a time that was so desperately filled with
the questioning of my continued existence

and now your ray of inspirational light has me blushing
and your words of inspirational insight have me gushing
and your toys of inspirational delight have me rushing
home to lay next to you

and so I want to thank you
for endearingly listening to my dreams and wishes and fantasies
for supporting my artistic endeavors
and for soothing the bumps and bruises suffered at the hands of a hostile
corporate work environment

you kept it all together through stormy weather and I could never imagine
that such supernatural strength lie behind such exquisite beauty

your willingness to please
and your willingness to indulge
and your willingness to oblige
damn, you just allow me to be all that I can be

so the sexual confidence that I now have is in great part because of you
and this raging thunder from down under is ALL because of you
so please don't deny your visual inspection
come hither, come slither, and orally confirm this visible erection

now take your time and do what I taught you
as you've practiced enough with the toys that I've bought you
and I'll do the same and I'll savor your wine
as we slowly and thoroughly enjoy a 69

your verbal induced applause
caused by my herbal induced jaws
is forcing me to hesitantly withdraw
sweet tasting sticky juice from your favorite straw

ooooooohhhhhhh!!!! aaaaaaahhhhhh!!!! yyyyyeeeeesssss!!!! I just want to
thank you

Happy Anniversary, Baby!

My, my, my
Where has the time gone?
It's been **365 days** since
I said what I said.
It's been **8,765.81277 hours** since
you said what you said
It's been **525,948.766 minutes** since
we did what we did in front of witnesses
declaring our love, honor and cherishment for each other.
And since then, there's been
endless positions attempted
AND
continuous improvements made
AND
continual destruction of
bedframes,
countertops,
tabletops,
bathroom sinks,
shower curtains,
rail banisters,
movie seats,
department store dressing rooms,
airport stalls,
airplane lavatories,
emptied zoo caves,
-or so we thought-
It's been **31,566,926 seconds** since
we said "I do!"
and I just wanted to let you know that I'm looking forward to all the new
places and adventures of the next

31,566,926 seconds
525,948.766 minutes
8,765.81277 hours

365 days
including leap year
Happy Anniversary, Baby!

Syllabus
SEX 069: Seminar in Maximizing Your Orgasm
Summer 2006

Location

1445 Brentwood Terrace, Master Bedroom Suite

Instructor

Walee FeelSoGood, Ph.D.
Associate Professor of Human Sexuality
Director of Service-Learning
New Jersey Institute of Sexual Technology
908-822-7015 ext 69
walee@att.net

Introduction to Course

The need and search for sexual fulfillment has rendered too many individuals physically, monetarily, emotionally, and mentally exhausted and frustrated. This seminar is designed to acquaint undergraduate students with some of the basic principles and theories of orgasm management and instructional practices associated with achieving such. This information applies without regard to age, gender or sexual identity. This seminar will include field trips, readings, lectures, discussions, and individual and group activities.

You have registered for the class "A Seminar In Maximizing Your Orgasm." Please review and sign the release form relieving Professor Walee of any liability due to excessive mental, emotional or physical scarring you may experience during or at the conclusion of this sexercise. A hands-on course, you will learn by participating in a variety of shape shifting positions which should generate greater pelvic access, exposure, and release of tension (including fluids). Many of the demonstrated skills could prove extremely hazardous if done incorrectly as they involve flight, inversion and unusual positions, any of which could result in serious injury, paralysis or death.[2] On the flip side, it could also result in jubilation, orchestral screaming and slaps of your Mama.

Course Objectives

At the successful completion of this course, students will prepare a portfolio demonstrating mastery of the following course objectives:

1. Articulate a philosophy of teaching your partner(s) how, when, and where to please you.

2. Develop performance based objectives and a course syllabus with required components so that you may go forth and teach your own Orgasm Management Course.

3. Develop assessment and evaluation techniques based on sound pedagogical principles which will result in the enhanced performance of your partner(s).

4. Demonstrate the ability to design and deliver an effective *oral* lecture presentation.

5. Articulate and develop various role playing learning methods to keep things stimulating and exciting and new.

6. Integrate pleasure inducing toys into instructional activities.

Required Texts

A. Blue, Violet (2002) <u>The Ultimate Guide to Fellatio: How to Go Down on a Man and Give Him Mind-Blowing Pleasure (Ultimate Everything!!!)</u>. San Franscisco: Cleis Press

---

2   www.drillsandskills.com

B. Blue, Violet (2002) <u>The Ultimate Guide To Cunnilingus: How to Go Down on a Woman and Give Her Exquisite Pleasure (Ultimate Everything!!!)</u>. San Francisco: Cleis Press

C. Fox, Randy (2004) <u>Sex 101: 101 Positions To Add Spice To Your Sex Life</u>. New York: Hylas Publishing.

D. Fox, Randy (2004) <u>Advanced Sex: 99 Positions for the Sexually Adventurous</u>. New York: Hylas Publishing.

E. Milligan, Rosie (1994) <u>Satisfying the Black Man Sexually Made Simple</u>. California: Professional Business Consultants

F. T., Miss (2005) <u>The Guide to Becoming the Sensuous Black Woman (And Drive Your Man Wild in and Out of Bed!)</u>. New Jersey: Oshun Publishing Company

Examinations

Why oral, of course!

I'm going to wear you out!

1. Flavored, scented, and glow-in-the-dark boxes of Condoms

2. Erotic devices for pent up vices (French Ticklers; Vibrators; Dildos; Feathers; Leather Harnesses; Blindfolds; Bondage Gear; DVDs; lingerie and costumes)

3. Defibrillator

4. Portable oxygen unit

5. Resuscitators

6. Cool Gel

7. Personal Antimicrobial Wipes (100/box)

8. Sterile Eye Pads

9. Body Fluid Cleanup Kit with PPE

10. 24-pack Poland Spring Water

11. Cool towels

12. Smelling salts

13. 911 on speed dial

14. Let the games begin

Chapter 2

The Main Course

A pen is the tool that I use to write.
A penis is the tool that I use to make things right.
Walee

Don't you remember you told me you loved me?
Where were you when I needed you most?

Whatever you do, don't look him in the eyes.
Ooh, ooh, child, things are gonna get freakier.

Jackie's Jook Joint
It's the place where all the happy people go.

Bigger is better, isn't it?
You tell me.

Don't you remember you told me you loved me?

Saturday, October 1, 2005, 5:00 p.m. This is the moment I've been anticipating for the past 30 days. I trained for this evening like it was a heavyweight championship fight. An early morning Dion Johnson Extreme Marine Boot Camp Class to leave me with a nightfall golden glow? Check! A Jamaican Dave haircut to accentuate the subtle waves? Check! Brushed teeth and peppermints handy? Check! Understated attire that oozed sensuality? Check! A Montblanc writing pen? Check! Well then, let's get this party started!

I arrive at the book signing destination, Sienna Visions Art Gallery[3] in Plainfield, New Jersey. Unbeknownst to me, gallery co-owner, Cydnie, and caterer extraordinaire, Shanda, had prepared a Walee Wall of Fame which consisted of my pictures and excerpts from my literary debut, *Confession is Good for the Soul: Lyrics of Love, Lullabies of Pain.* In spite of being in the best physical condition of my life, my legs grew weak and wobbly as I took in the picturesque wall complimented with paintings by the gallery's co-owner, world-renowned painter, Alonzo Adams.

As one who is never at a loss for words, for one of the very few times in my life I was speechless. I hugged and squeezed the ladies so hard that I think I may have cracked a rib or two. There was no need for me to stay at the gallery any longer. There was no way that this overwhelming feeling could become any more powerful. I would soon realize how wrong I was. At 6:00 p.m. *they* entered the gallery. One by one they came, family, friends, and internet acquaintances who all found the time to share in this most memorable occasion. I was shocked by the distance that some traveled *(cousins Virgil & Peaches, OHS sweetheart, Maria Webster, Kiesha Hooks-Lee, and Mr. International himself, Bill Freeman)* and could not believe that my forearm could actually be so tired from signing my name and anecdotes to the many book purchasers, 104 in fact.

---

3   www.siennavisions.com

Around 8:30 p.m., it was determined that the crowd capacity was at its maximum and that it was time for my performance. My dearest high school friend, *Veronica Fryer*, now married and known as *Veronica Clemons*, had agreed to be one of the female perspective readers. She performed *Don't Say Goodbye, Say Goodnight* to great applause. I thanked her with a big bear hug and took the center of the floor to give them what they really came for-ALL OF ME! I opened with *Signed Sealed and Delivered with a Kiss* followed by *Happy Birthday, Baby* followed by *The Greatest Love of All* and ended with *You Don't Feel the Way I Feel about You*. I made eye contact with every person in the audience and could tell by their grins, gasps and sighs that I was on point and making the intended connection. By the time I finished reading the last stanza of *You Don't Feel The Way I Feel About You*, I felt like a rock star. The delirium reached such decibels that I felt my eardrums pounding as the applause was deafening and lengthy.

I got more hugs, kisses, squeezes, and pats than at all of the combined orgies I've ever participated. OK, joke, joke but seriously, the demonstrative affection was stupendous. As we departed the gallery, well after 10:30 p.m. *(wasn't this event supposed to be over at 9:00 p.m.?)* I headed to the home of my Spiritual Guru, Rajabu, where I was feted with the most appreciative after party. Good fun was had by all. There are plenty of blackmail pictures to prove it! I finally made my way home to fall asleep around 4:30 a.m. I closed my eyes and internally confessed that if I didn't wake up as the sun rose early the next day, I would die knowing glorious peace and awesome wonder. The previous night's experience was truly unforgettable.

In a review of the event, **Solomon Valentino** wrote that "...Walee, he of the massive fist pumps and megawatt smile, bowed his head and drew his hand over his heart as his adoring friends, family, and fans showered him with a thunderous ovation acknowledging that confession is indeed good for the soul..."

Wow, I smiled. And then a shocking moment grasped my heart, my intellect, my Cancerian sensitive nature. **You weren't there!** The greatest moment I had in years and you were not there to share it with me. Others didn't show too and I shook uncontrollably as I mentally replayed the evening while cross referencing the RSVP list and acknowledging the non-attendees. I checked voice and e-mail messages hoping, wishing, even praying that all was well and nothing tragic had happened. There were no messages and I became incensed. After all I've done *and* given *and* provided *and* paid for, you would think that…I got on my knees and begged for forgiveness as my evil twin personality, Jean-Luc, was about to erupt and kick all kinds of ass. No, I will not revert back to that demonic personality. I've accomplished so much and would not risk it by doing something so stupid. But truth be told, I wanted to exact revenge.

Thanks to some sage advice from my darling, *Jackie Young*, I was reminded that my ultimate goal was to surpass the expectations of those who **did** attend. I firmly believe that was accomplished. **Jackie** also reminded me that not everyone would or could be happy for me and that not everyone would be able to join me on my new journey. While I was saddened at the thought, I have come to realize that she was telling the truth. It has been four months since I've heard from any of those who had RSVPd affirmatively but did not come. But all of their absences combined could not hurt me more yours. I thought you knew me, I mean really, really knew me. I guess you don't really know me at all. Or maybe you do and you knowingly and willingly set out to disappoint me. You couldn't possibly be jealous of me, could you? Do you have any idea how much I love you? I guess it's not reciprocal. You have yet to attend any of my book events or even comment on my webpage or book signing pictures.

I wish you God speed and nothing but continued success in your personal and professional endeavors. I strongly recommend that you buy a pair of the latest Ray-Ban sunglasses. You'll need them to block the radiant energy pouring out of my very soul. Don't you remember you told me you loved me? Well, if you really love me, then show it! Prove it! State it! Represent it!

Whatever you do, don't look him in the eyes

By day, he's Corporate Man. You can find him attired in a Brooks Brothers suit, a Kilgour French & Stansbury shirt, Johnston and Murphy wing tips, Christian Dior scent, hmmm…Yeah, this bespectacled brutha is doing the damn thing:

- Developing quarterly reports for board meetings, analyst's reviews and shareholder results

- Shattering stereotypes and destroying myths

His business acumen is the foundation for The Donald's <u>Apprentice</u>. For all his Wall Street savvy, he's a gentlemen, scholar and overall nice guy to have fun with. He's witty but can't cook at all. The poor thing burns boiling water, yet his dance moves are legendary! You MUST see him perform his Batman step☺

This is all the reason why I'm so bent out of shape and can't exactly explain how it happened. You see, we were working late one night at his place as we have done on many occasions, and then I woke up. Not that I was asleep, mind you, but somehow my consciousness became unconscious and I awoke feeling euphoric, slightly unbalanced and curiously moist. I see his lips move but I don't hear a sound as I'm trying to confirm this vaguely familiar twinge between my thighs. Unfortunately, it's been a while since I've tasted some Duncan Hines chocolate, if you know what I mean. But I know how I feel when I…and I damn sure know how I smell when I…Oh my gosh, what the hell has happened?

He's still talking and I'm nodding in agreement while examining the loft space for clues of where and what has apparently occurred. Intense concentration and recollection of thought slowly reveal what has transpired, and I'm transfixed at the slow motion video my mind's eye rolls out before me.

He took his glasses off. It was just that simple. He took his glasses off, and his eyes, his beautiful brown eyes looked at me with such sincerity, such intensity, such adulation that I'm telling you, girl, one moment we're calculating spreadsheets and the next moment he has me spread eagle across his bedsheets.

I don't know how I got there. We were simply reviewing the schematics and he tilted his glasses to rub his eyes, and the next thing I know he's lapping and munching between my thighs.

He was merely explaining the numbers behind the numbers with the simplest of ease. The next thing I know is that he adjusted his rims, and I'm immediately servicing him from down on my knees.

Tyleef, our favorite pizza delivery man, had arrived, and Corporate Man and I are supposed to be paying Dutch. But one flick of his rims and there's no orifice that he, and Tyleef, has not touched.

Yes, Tyleef too was immediately impacted by looking directly into Corporate Man's eyeglass-missing irises. He dropped the pizza on the floor, then dropped himself to all fours, and began panting and pacing as he made his way to my now unrestricted breasts. When did my blouse come off? When did my bra come off? When did Tyleef take his pants off? When did my panties come off?

Motown's 1's competes for audible attention as a myriad of sensual sighs and aria highs fill the air. There's nowhere to run and nowhere to hide as Marvin's now moaning about his needing and wanting and gotta have some sexual healing. I was once told that two women and a man together is a beautiful thing called a ménage a trios, and that two men and a woman together is simply called a train. Well, somebody better call the conductor because I did not pay for this ticket to ride. Diana's now singing about how she don't want it, that she don't need no cure for this. I agree totally as every nook and cranny of my body was being teased, tasted, and tossed.

An old TV jingle was being sung by the two of them, "Hold the pickle, hold the lettuce, special orders don't upset us…have it your way." Special is how I felt, and I did have it my way as these sexual symbioses lovingly obliged all requests to sample my nipples, fingers, toes, labia, earlobes, tongue, and belly button. My internal conductor announces, "Next stop, Orgasmica Orchard!" and I scream out, "Pull up to my bumper, baby, and park it in between!" Wait, that's not on the Motown 1's CD but I don't care as Junior Walker and the All Stars take me home with, "Shotgun, shoot em for he runs now…"

"Yes, PapiChulo, shoot me with your love right now 'cause I'm not looking for Mr. Right, I'm looking for Mr. Right Now, some Mandingo, spear-carrying, dick-swinging-from-Malaysia-to-Miami brutha who ain't afraid to eat from my passion fruit and to deep fuck me into a bliss-ridden coma. Oh, let's get it on cause I've got to give it up!" I'm now hearing Sam and Dave's "Hold on, I'm coming, hold on, I'm coming!" That too ain't on the soundtrack but what the hell, mission accomplished!!!"

And then it was over. Just like that. I was awake and this time for real as I looked directly into those beautiful brown eyes as Corporate Man asks, "Are you OK? You appear to be flushed."

"Yes, I'm OK, it's just that crunching all these damn numbers has given me a headache, and I need a lil tension release. How about a pizza? Ooh, with pepperoni and sausages!"

Corporate Man says, "Sure, I'll call Dominico's and request my man Tyleef to deliver. Care for some Kendall Jackson?"

"Yeah, I could sure use a glass."

I slightly turn my head to conceal an iniquitous grin as I think about that fine azz Tyleef, and how I've longed wished to wash his manhood with my salacious saliva. I gingerly fall back onto the lush leather couch and throw my arms up in the air and rest them around the back of my neck, exposing my honey melons.

"By the way, do you have any Motown in your collection?"

Jackie's Jook Joint

A song lyric goes,
"...all the lonely people, where do they all come from...[4]"

I don't know where they come from
but I do know where they go...
to Jackie's Jook Joint.

they come to hear sonnets of symphonies
mellifluous melodies,
and tonight's special, Love Notes 2 A Black Man.

Damn, I've been at this urinal for about a minute now trying to release a much needed pisser. One hand on my Johnson and the other holding myself up against the wall, I admire the sophomoric linguistic expressions scattered across the tattered wallpaper. "For a good time, call 1-800-CALL-A-FK...1-800-FK-ME-NOW...1-800-HORNYME...1-800-WHO-D-MAN." 1-800-EATMEUP...1-800-SUCKME2..." Just as my eyes were about to read the wall's second verse, HotsieTwatsie Cherry Drop, stumbles out of the stall rapidly wiping her mouth as she coughs up cum onto the pee-stained floor. Crazy ass Junebug staggers out immediately afterwards looking at me through a half-closed right eye, as if he done hit the jackpot. The nigga definitely has an oral fixation. Just yesterday he went out and got two blow jobs then came back and tried to give me one. He owed me money, couldn't pay up so he offered and I disrespectfully declined by blacking his eye.

Truth be told, this dick aint been hard in years. I fucked around and waited too long to get this prostate cancer shit checked out and treated; and when I did, the cure left me alive yet impotent. An occasional exception is when I hear Jackie do her thing. By golly, that woman can sure stir

---

[4]   Eleanor Rigby by Paul McCartney and John Lennon

up some long denied feelings. Dammit, come on now, I plead with my Johnson. She should be on any minute. Hesitantly, a slow stream of yellow piss finally releases itself from Daddy Long-Long and I sigh, comforted in knowing that maybe I'll be finished in time to see Jackie walk on stage. I zip up, wash my hands and leave the bathroom, hearing plans for an encore performance between HotsieTwatsie and Junebug. If I've missed Jackie's opening number, I'm gonna have to blacken Junebug's other eye.

Entering the small, non-descript lounge, I see the regulars: Princess Dom with her calves pumped and juicy-looking due to her 4-inch Manolo Blahnik Open Toe Mary Janes…Mr. Marcus…Black Diamond…Thunderbird Tim…Shake-A-Boom Shai, Too-Tuff Tzynya…Miss "Don't Make Me Stab My Husband" TJ…VoomVoom VeeJay…Straight-No Chaser-Mocha… Purified Pittershawn…Hush, Hush, Sweet Charlotte…Call Her Miss TC…Pretty Peggy…Edgy Evelyn…Cryptic Carla…and a host of ole heads and newbies all looking to get their literary groove on. I give high fives to the bruthas and approach the ladies' table hoping to be enveloped with oversized, aged or sagging breasts, the kind that deliciously nurtured triplets. Alas, the women here know too much about my freaky azz and offer air kisses punctuated with sucks of their teeth and rolling of their eyes.

"What's happening with you this evening, brutha man, and more importantly, what are you drinking?" asks Brian, the bartender.

"Well, you know that I am too blessed to be stressed and too anointed to be disappointed, but right here and right now, I gots me the blues and I needs a drink! Some of my best friends begin with the letter J so give me three drinks…Jack Daniels, Jim Bean Black and Johnny Walker Red."

"Damn, man, is it that bad?"

"You don't know the half of it. If Jackie doesn't drown out my sorrows this evening, I'll be back for a triple shot of arsenic. I'm sick and tired of being sick and tired!"

"Ladies and Gentlemen, welcome to Jackie's Jook Joint. Let's kick off tonight's entertainment with our opening act, Like2LickULenny."

"Wassup, e'rybody? I just wanna drop a li'l somethin', somethin', I call Silly Shit."

Honesty Is The Best Policy

I don't trust that bitch, Victoria. She's got secrets. **Ba-dum-Bum!**

A Lil Something About Me

I've had more butts than your silver ashtray
I've given more dicktation than most secretaries can scribe
I've taken more bullshit than a plumber can plunge
I've received more offers of head than a psychiatrist can examine…**Ba-dum-Bum!**

Season's Greetings

Ho, Ho, Ho…my sleigh bells are ringing
So, So, So…down her chimney I am bringing
Mo, Mo, Mo…gifts a blinging, dick a swinging
Go, Go, Go…deeper and faster, an eruption is springing
No, No, No…A shot of penicillin to alleviate the stinging…**Ba-dum-Bum!**

Holiday…Celebrate…

Whereas a nut resting on the wall is called a walnut,
and a nut resting on a chest is called a chestnut,
and a nut resting on a chin is called a dick in your mouth,
I hereby proclaim today National SuckADick Day…**Ba-dum-Bum, Ching!**

"Thank you, thank you, you've been far too kind…"

Polite applause is provided as Like2LickULen makes his way around the bar shaking hands and receiving pats on his firm back from the bruthas and pats on his firm ass from the sistas.

"...ohhhh, it's been such a long, long time, seems like I can't get you off my mind..."

"Nobody wants to hear that damn Misty Blue shit!
Where the hell is Jackie?
When is she coming on?
When will she ease the pain?
and
remove the strain on this lonely man's heart?
This heart that is simply looking for love
in all the wrong places
Jackaaaaayyyyy??? Jackaaaayyyy? Where you at?
Get your ass out here and put it on me, woman
Whip me into a dizzying frenzy with your literary lasso
Transport me to that mystical and mythical island called Jacquelina
where the mangos are sweet but not as sweet as the island's namesake
and
where the natives are pretty but not as pretty as the island's namesake
and
where you can pontificate and pick of poetic passion fruit that are ripe and juicy and savory
but none as much as the island's namesake

though this evening's crowd consist of many
she speaks to directly to me
through me
later tonight her poetic hocus pocus will result in my own orgasmal opus
but for now, right now, at this moment
I am imprisoned by the anticipation of her voice
Her truth

Her justice
Her affirmations
Her…"

"Damn, nigga, shut the fuck up and sit your drunk ass down!"

"I am not drunk, dammit, and I will not shut the fuck up!
Jackaaaaaayyyyy, Jackaaaaayyyy, where you at?
It's me, baby, don't you hear me calling?
Don't you see me falling
down
and
picking
myself up
just to hear you deliver emotive epiphanies
I want you to
          Surround me with a sonic sonata
               Crush me with a concerto
                    Beat me with your…
                         Smack me with your…
                              Slap me with your…
                                   Strangle me with your…"

"There she is…Here she comes, y'all!"

Jackie walks through the crowd resplendent in lavender Jamaican haute couture. It appears that the moon is no longer in the seventh house, and Jupiter is no longer aligned with Mars as the heavenly constellations realign themselves competing to illuminate her beauty. Corona Borealis and Ursa Minor make a pact and gang up on Canis Major and Canes Venatici for a front row position. And speaking of positions, at the sight of Jackie, Daddy Long-Long is suddenly getting fidgeting and is competing with Inspector 12's fruit of the looms' boxer briefs for his own front row view. Oh boy! Looka here! Can I sustain it? Can I restrain it? Can I contain it?

"Good evening, everyone. My name is Jackie. Let's start tonight with a *Striptease*[5]."

One incredible journey after another, Jackie takes the audience on a literary kaleidoscopic roller coaster ride. Peaks and valleys, crescendos and accelerandos, cadenza and allargando were all magically weaved together creating a transcendent experience for the audience.

I yell out, "I told you her arsenal was stocked with all kinds of detonations of desire! Jackie's Jook Joint is now officially jumpin!"

Filled, half-filled, and empty glasses are thrown to the floor and wondrous wails of exhilaration are released as the crowd erupts with claps more powerful than a Thor thunderbolt. And speaking of Thor, his wife Sif, the fertility Goddess, must be shaking her fantail because a feverish fervor is permeating the small cramped quarters. In paying respect to tonight's spoken word title, clothes are beginning to be peeled off, some ripped off, and some jumped out of all in sync to Diana Ross' Love Hangover.

A song lyric goes, "…all the lonely people, where do they all come from…"
I don't know where they come from
but I sure do know where they go…to Jackie's Jook Joint.

---

[5] For more about Jackie, please visit www.soulfullsoliloquies.blogspot.com

Bigger is better, isn't it?

I have penis envy. No, I'm not gay, bi-sexual, bi-curious, on the down low or any other term used to describe men who engage in sexual activity of any type with other men. I'm short changed downstairs…I'm physically challenged below…dammit, I have a lil dick! There, I've said it. Are you happy?

There are no recollections of childhood distance pissing challenges or show me yours and I'll show you mine games. Thus I had no idea that I was *challenged* in the area of penile length and width. I do recall that the prior to elementary school graduation it was explained that in junior high school, students are required to take showers after participating in gym class. No big deal I thought as this was just another way to demonstrate that I wasn't a little kid anymore. I had begun growing fuzz under my arms and around my genital area. Always hearing about the restorative powers of Dixie Peach in making the hair on one's head grow, I ingeniously thought that I would start applying Dixie Peach *downstairs* and would brush, brush, and brush hoping that the hair would grow faster. I wanted a mini afro by the time junior high school began, and I thought of the boastful pride I would flex when it came down to shower time.

Junior high begins and it's quite different from elementary school. As the only such school in the city, all the elementary schools send their graduating 6th graders there. Looking throughout the auditorium for any familiar face, I'm awestruck with how everyone has grown so much over the summer. Everybody seemed so much taller, heavier, and more fashionably dressed. Dang, some of my friends were even sporting early traces of mustaches! Major anxieties started settling in as I was still wearing what was considered last year's clothing. When did "Swedish Knits" become *the* pants to wear? When did Buster Brown shoes become *the* shoes for the little kids? When did cursing become *so* cool? When did kissing girls in public become *so* acceptable? I was beginning to not like this thing called junior high. I wanted to go back to the comfort of 6th grade where, like the TV show Cheers, everybody knew my name. Now with a nappy afro, Pro-

Keds sneakers, and not being able to afford to go out to lunch—yeah, I was stigmatized with the dreaded lunch card—I felt like I had to start all over again building up my rep.

The auditorium was cleared and all students received their schedules which outlined which classes and room numbers that we'd changed to throughout the day. Each class period found students getting to know each other better with alliances quickly being formed based on family income, neighborhood residence, *skin tone*, and test score results to name a few. The bell rings and its fourth period, time for Physical Education.

We're assigned lockers to store our changed clothes and begin every kid's favorite gym sport, dodgeball. Whereby I used to be able to throw with striking accuracy and strength, the enhanced physical bodies of my new peers allowed them to be able to dodge all my throws yet strike me with such accuracy that my tan colored skin was now black and blue. The whistle blows and the teachers yells, "Off to the showers!" I think to myself, "Yeah, I'll show them who's boss now!" as my Dixie Peached, brushed 25 times a day pubic hair is waiting for its showcase debut. I enter my combination number to open my lock. As I look to the right of me, Eddie is already undressed and carrying an appendage that surely cannot be what I think it is. What the fuck??? The head. The length. The veins. This just can't be possible. I'm trying not to stare but my eyes are transfixed as the site of his massive shaft.

"Hurry up guys and get it done as you need to be outta here in 5 minutes!" yells the gym teacher as an exodus of bodies head toward the showers.

Now surrounded by at least 9 other pre-puberscent punks, the chastising game began.

"Look at that, he don't got no hair down there. Whassup with that, pussy boy?"

"Look at that, he got an ass shaped like a girl!"

"Look at that, where's your dick, boy? I aint never seen anything that small before except on my lil baby brother and he's five years old!"

One by one a few of us were being selected and pounced upon with verbal humiliation. I'm hoping and praying that the rising steam from the collective heated waters would minimize some visibility and that there'd be no comment on my *limitation* but alas I wasn't spared. As Bernard was about to say something fucked up, Teacher yells out, "Alright, fellas, get outta here. Next 10 up now!"

Whew! I got lucky, or so I thought. I then realized that unlike elementary school, we now have gym every day of the week. This was going to be a long year.

One by one we run out of the shower and head toward our respective lockers to dry off. Lamont's on my left, Cameron's in back of me towards my right, and PJ's on his left. I'm surrounded by inches and inches of dick, and I feel an uneasiness growing in my stomach. I'm hoping and praying that they don't start cracking on me and my *lil man* and then Eddie walks up to the locker.

"Hey, hurry up, cuz. We got pre-Algebra next period and I don't want to be late." He looked at the others and gave them a menacing look that clearly meant that I was not to be messed with. Good ole Cousin Eddie was always coming to my rescue. Our fathers were brothers but after seeing his *third leg* I was beginning to believe that I was adopted.

"I'll be right with you…just gotta lace up my sneakers."

From the next row, Lance snickers, "Skits don't grip, take em off…"

Before I could respond, Cousin Eddie had already snatched Lance by the collar and had him pinned up against the locker. "You fuck with him, you get fucked up by me, UNDERSTOOD???"

"Yeah, yeah, I was just joking, damn!" sniffles a teary-eyed Lance.

Teacher yells again, "Didn't I tell you guys to hurry up and get outta here? Move it, darn it, right fast and right now." We slam locker doors and hustled our way out.

After about two weeks the cliques were complete. You had those who played sports, those who excelled academically, the troublemakers, and the light skinned with *good* hair crew to name a few of those that stood out the most. However, the most noted was the BDC (Big Dick Club). It didn't matter if you could play ball well, got all A's, or lived in the ritzy Seven Oaks section. If there was ever a verbal dispute and a BDC guy was losing and about to face defeat, he would throw down his trump card, "But *MY* dick is *BIGGER* than *YOURS*, mutherfucker!" Such an argument could always be counted on to end with that statement and the recipient of this vocal assault would plummet back to his chair defeated, embarrassed, and humiliated. The other BDC members would roar with thunderous laughter and jeer while those of us *less fortunate* would slowly shrink in our seats hoping that we wouldn't be exposed as the roaring hilarity grew louder and louder.

Once, Jimbo got called out and Snookie erred by participating in the raucous laughter. The BDC did not appreciate Snookie joining in their amusement. When the school bell rang signaling the day's end, the BDC cornered Snookie, stripped him of his pants and shit-stained underwear, threw them out of the hall window and forced him to walk to his locker exposing his exceptionally small boyhood wonder. The girls pointed and whooped. Other guys too afraid to demonstrate their horror reluctantly joined in the teasing knowing that their turn could be one day soon.

Snookie never returned to school and the BDC got away with their persecution as no one would reveal who did what for fear of the BDC's reprisal.

That first marking period found me exploring so many ways attempting to lengthen my male embarrassment. I read *EVERYTHING* about suction pumps, pills and surgery whereby they cut, stretch and stitch the penis with promises of gaining 3 to 5 inches of growth. All these options seemed very plausible and I wanted to act on them but being twelve years old and poor didn't leave me much choice.

The rest of junior high was spent dealing with acne and other pre-teen issues but most important was my issue with penile length. While more blood was finding its way into my often swollen erections thus giving the illusion that it had gotten bigger, in its limp phase, I clearly did not quality enough to submit an application to the BDC.

Junior high graduation led to high school and basically it was more of the same-cliques, fashion statements, and my pre-occupation with increasing the size of my dick. While there was more hair under my arms and around my genital area including my ass (what's that about?) my dick didn't grow nearly as large as my peers' or to my expectation. Before hitting the showers I would go to the bathroom and work a jerk, let it subside and head off to wash up hoping that the enhanced version would somewhat compete. Alas, it was not the case.

Still running interference when he needed to, Cousin Eddie was always there not knowing that he was fueling an increasingly internal rage and insecurity. We once got busy with big butt Brenda Boone. Actually, he got busy. I just got to taste her titties and in the middle of doing so made a nasty mess on her pretty dress. Dejected and horrified by her response, I sat back and watched Cousin Eddy make Brenda squirm and squeal with glee. Extended plunges led to collapsed lungs and moans. Such harmonious moans echoed throughout the room. And as I watched, I focused not on Brenda but on Cousin Eddie's dick. Watching as it grew bigger.

Watching as it went in and out of Brenda hands, her mouth, and then her vagina. Watching as it erupted, spraying itself all over Brenda's face. Watching as he gave her a penile facial, rubbing it back and forth and around and around until it dried and she clapped her hands exclaiming "Bravo, baby, bravo!" And I watched as it grew smaller and smaller but still bigger and apparently better than what I carried between my legs. And at that moment our French word of the day, **bête noire**, became more meaningful as Cousin Eddie's dick had become the thing that I most particularly disliked. I swore that something was awry in my family lineage in spite of my sudden growth spurt that now had us looking eye to eye. We both grew up eating at Big Ma's on Sundays. I could easily beat him at all running games and was definitely smarter than him. So why was *he* the one blessed with the big dick and not me?

The BDC membership had now expanded due to the extra grade levels but their ridicule and torment was not like it was in junior high school. If anything, the girls were more promiscuous and brazen. Vanity 6's "I need seven inches or more" and Adena's "freak like me" flowed from their lips easily and forthright.

Thanks to a spike in puberty, I made the JV basketball team because of my newfound height and now was able to hang around some of the more popular people. I even was able to get a girlfriend, Vanessa Daniels. Our relationship was very short as during a making out session she felt and grabbed and pulled and tugged and didn't find *enough* to her liking. She was cool though, no offending remarks or belittling. She just wanted something bigger to *play* with. We remained friendly throughout high school. In fact it was her older sister Angela that took my virginity. Apparently, Vanessa explained to Angela that the reason why we weren't dating anymore is because of my size, or lack thereof. Angela saw in me what most teenage girls don't readily see, potential.

Being with Angela was the best experience of my life. She was patient, all-knowing and slightly older. OK, 10 years older. She taught me how to relax and to stop pounding like I was a jackhammer. She taught me about lines and angles and penetration spots that even a man of my *stature* could use to ensure her gratification. She taught me that it wasn't about my pleasure but about hers. She showed me where the erogenous zones were and about the power of a good tongue tickle, as she called it. Angela most valuable teaching lesson was showing me how to work with what I had and to make up for what I didn't by using my newly discovered secret weapon, my tongue. Who knew that it could compete on equal footing for providing pleasure, holding its own against *lil man*. Angela confirmed that my tongue should be certified as a second-degree black belt in the art of pussy eating. I absolutely adore licking labia, muff munching, carpet cleaning, deep sea diving…No matter what you call it, I love eating it!

Thanks to Angela, I was able to overcome my *size inhibition* anxieties and really enjoy the rest of my high school years. Though she and Vanessa moved mid-way through my junior year, she instilled great confidence in me and I truly came to understand that there was more power in pleasing a woman than waiting to receive pleasure from one. Not that she was tricked out or anything, but after getting real good with using my *secret oral weapon*, I was able to get those Converse All Star sneaks and those Swedish Knits pants. Although it could have been that she just got a great sale because no one was wearing that shit anymore.

Ultimately, high school graduation led to college graduation which led to full time employment which led to significant weight gain which led to high blood pressure, cholesterol and doctor's orders to exercise more and to lose weight if I wanted to live a lot longer. At his urging, I joined the local gym.

The facility is thoroughly modern yet the shower set up takes me back to junior high as it's an all-open area. As you enter, you're bound to witness someone starting, in the middle of or ending their washup. Whether it's an ass, oversized belly or a long dick, short dick, thick dick, uncircumsized dick, pierced dick…you name it, I've seen it. And upon seeing it, I consciously compare and contrast myself, my value, and my worth. You would think that after all the success I've accomplished to date-a beautiful wife, three adoring children, a great entrepreneurial empire-that I would be mentally and emotionally secure enough not to feel inadequate when it comes down to the size of my penis. Alas, I'm still struggling.

Most men I know think that big breasts represent beauty and femininity. The pressure for a lot of today's women singers and actresses to enhance their boobies is very prevalent. Bigger is better, isn't it? While Hollywood's plastic surgeons' offices are filled with countless beauties waiting their turn for impeccable enhancements, there's a great amount of attention being drawn to those surgeries that have gone awry. Most notably for me was Toni Braxton whose implant ruptured causing internal poisoning, sickness and had to be removed.

And on the other end of the spectrum, I read how Queen Latifah opted to get her breast sized reduced due to constant back and neck pain. Other side effects of massive mammories include gouges in a woman's shoulders from bra straps, deteriorating posture and an inability to participate in certain activities. If this is case, do you think I should feel sorry for some of gym shower brethren? Do you think their big dicks are causing them lower back and abdominal strain, groin injuries, or swollen testicles? And hey, if the average depth of a woman's vagina is 3 to 6 inches, where are all those extra inches going? And if most women aren't technically skilled to successfully compete with Karrine "Superhead" Steffans (she's the hip hop version of yesteryear's Linda Lovelace's Deep Throat for all you ole heads freaks like me), where is all those extra inches going? By golly, is all that extra packaging being wasted, just hanging around and not getting any attention except for an occasional lick on the way to the head? Wow, I never really thought about it like that. Suddenly, I'm feeling empowered. At least I can get *all* of mine in and work it to orgasmic perfection for us both. Aaaaawwww, so sad for them I am. Tsk, tsk, all that dick and the best thing they can do is to take matters into you're their own hands. Shucks! But wait. If gravity gets us all at life's end—drooping eyes and sagging breasts and hanging stomach—does this mean that by the age of 70 my Mini Me could morph into Long Dong Kong?

As you can see, my mind's a little twisted, and I apparently have way too much free time on my hands. We all make up coping mechanisms to assist with our feelings of inadequacies. My shero, Lauryn Hill, says, "Why for you to increase, I must decrease, and if I treat you kindly does it mean that I'm weak?"[6] I'm often haunted by occasional flashbacks of seeing Cousin Eddie, PJ, Lamont, Cameron and Len for the first time. I look downwards and sometimes curse my genetic makeup. Then I think of Angela and I smile. She said, "Use what you got to get what you want!" My tongue swells and so does my dick causing me to rush out of the gym's shower and head to the bathroom until the engorgement subsides. Dr. Trevor Forbes, my psychiatrist, says there's nothing wrong or strange about me. I simply have penis envy.

---

[6] The Miseducation of Lauryn Hill

Chapter 3

The Desserts

It takes courage to push yourself to places that you have never been before…to test your limits…to break through barriers. And the day came when the risk it took to remain tight inside the bud was more painful than the risk it took to blossom.

Anais Nin

My Pride & Joy
So much confusion causes a cerebral contusion

Smootches
She's an original Write-or-Die Chic. If you can't be the poet, be the poem!

Imagine Me
I close my eyes and fantasize

I Don't Know What Else To Do
When is enough, enough?

I Never Can Say Goodbye
A Motown medley lingers on

How could you…?
Aint this some shit!

A Mother's Lament
>   It takes a fool to learn that...

For Miss Rosa
>   Rest now, our beloved guiding light

All I Ever Wanted
>   Be careful what you wish for

The Love We Had Stays On My Mind
>   I'll remember you forever...

My Pride & Joy

In rap, in dance, in essays, in paintings…
there is **JUST TOO MUCH DAMN EMPHASIS**
placed on my pride and joy

its size, its taste
what it can buy
and where it is placed

the star of the story,
it gives a rousing performance and yields
standing ovations
and offers of donations
and unwanted creations
and threats of castrations

the relentless admiration and fascination and expectation
concerns me
as you follow me
and offer to swallow me
for compensation

and out of desperation
I give in to the hesitation
and focus on my concentration
to deny you a liquid celebration

what exactly happens when I don't measure up to your myth
and Mr. Magic doesn't measure up to your expected width
I admit that sometimes I get a lil insecure
'cause my pride and joy is not 100% pure…MANDINGO

my true feelings, you continue to discard
and the headlines continue to bombard
with so much written and with so much discussed
I'm reminded of the new Stevie single and have to ask, so what's the fuss?

there is **JUST TOO MUCH DAMN EMPHASIS**
placed on my pride and joy

Smootches

Sensual, sizzling kisses

Making me feel like never before

Over and over I cry out your name

Only to realize that it's just a dream

Trying to let you know on Wednesdays that I'm falling for you

Care to take this journey with me?

Here's to the endless positions and possibilities

Eternally yours

Say my name, say my name

Imagine Me

I asked that she send me a picture of her. She responded, "You claim that you are a creative person. Imagine me."

And so I am now imagining…

Us together, sitting adjoined and signing copies of our New York Times best sellers
> Us together, posing for paparazzi
>> Us together, waving to fans passing by as we cruise away in our stretch limo

Us together, sharing French champagne and Russian caviar and Godiva chocolates
> Us together, standing up in the limo yelling out, "We're King & Queen of the World!"
>> Us together, taking in the New York skyline as we head towards Trump Tower

Us together, holding hands, eyes engaged, smiling so mischeviously
> Us together, arriving at One Central Park West
>> Us together, exalting at the lobby's exquisiteness and securing our room keys

Us together, taking in the awesome wonder of our picturesque suite
> Us together, giving praise for our abundant blessings
>> Us together, calling family members to tell how beautiful the experience has been

Us together, undressing and hand-in-hand entering the jacuzzi
> Us together, soaking and laughing…washing and laughing…splashing and laughing

Us together, toweling, moisturizing, hair tending, and ordering exotic fruits via room service

Us together, squeezing citrus fruit juices onto select body parts
Us together, tasting squeezed juices off select body parts
Us together, squeezing select body parts unleashing orchestral moans and groans

Us together, becoming one as we put our Olympic gymnastic observations to sexual use
Us together, in the positions of Arch, Bridge, Candlestick, Handstand, Hollow
Us together engaging in more positions such as Pike, Planch, Straddle and Tuck

Us together,

until
we
have
simply
worn
each
other
out!
Oh, how I imagine thee…

Gymnastic Position Definitions[7]

Arch: In an arch a gymnast's hips are pushed forward, chest is open. Lie on your stomach with your arms by your ears. Lift your heels while keeping your legs straight, and lift your arms while keeping your arms straight.

---

7   www.drillsandskills.com

Bridge: A bridge is attained by lying on your back. Place your hands on the floor by your ears and bend your legs. Push your hips towards the ceiling and arch back. Ideally a bridge should have straight legs and shoulders pushed out over the hands.

Candlestick: A candle stick is a position where the gymnast is essentially standing on the back of their shoulders with their feet pointed towards the ceiling. The gymnasts arms can either be by their head, or back pushing on the floor to assist with support and balance.

Handstand: A proper handstand is extended towards the ceiling, shoulders are open, body is hollow.

Hollow: In a hollow a gymnast's hips are turned under, legs are tight chest rounded inward. Lie on your back on the floor with your arms by your ears. Lift your legs slightly off the ground. Lift your head slightly off the floor. Your lower back should maintain contact with the floor.

Pike: In a pike a gymnast is bent only at the hips. Sit on the floor with your legs straight out in front of you. Pikes of varying degrees including where a gymnast is esentially folded in half at their hips are used in gymnastics.

Planch: This is a handstand in which the body is parallel with the ground.

Straddle: In a straddle a gymnast's legs are separated with neither leg being forward or backward of the other. A straddled pike is a straddle in which the hips are closed or "piked" to some degree.

Tuck: In a tuck a gymnast is bend at the hips and the knees. Sit on the floor with your legs in front of you. Bend your knees so that your knees are touching your chest and your feet are "tucked" in close to your body. A variation on the tuck is called a "cowboy" tuck in which the gymnast pulls their knees out to the side somewhat in order to compress the tuck further. This enables faster rotation.

I Don't Know What Else To Do

like grains of sand
you're slipping through my hands
and I don't know what else to do

got me buying you shoes from Gucci
trying to act like you are Susan Lucci
and I don't know what else to do

simple conversations barely exist
tender affection you often resist
and I don't know what else to do

I want to do it doggie style but you won't comply
I want to do it froggie style but this request you deny
and I don't know what else to do

when did it become so complicated
why am I left to masturbate it
I don't know what else to do

should I call your girl, Sheila
should I try the corner dealer
'cause I don't know what else to do

options are running low
you've turned into someone I no longer know
and I don't know what else to do

do we continue to let this run its course
do you want to continue to ride that white horse
'cause I don't know what else to do

I've gotten the strength to walk out that door
look back at you once and then look back never more
'cause I finally know what's left to do

call 1-800-DIVORCE

I Never Can Say Goodbye

OK, it's over
I've accepted it
well, almost
not 100%
but I've concluded that it is me that you no longer wish to be married to
so go on ahead
you can break away from my grasp
AND
you can flee from our home
AND
you can leave me for him
AND
you can escape into his arms
BUT
Do not give him the look of joy when you awaken with him
    as you did with me
AND
Do not give him the nourishing breakfast to sustain him for an entire work
day
    as you did with me
AND
Do not give him the Josephine Baker nude banana-laced outfit as you
greet him from work
    as you did with me
AND
Do not give him the sweet wimpering sounds of orchestral orgasms when
you sexually exhale
    as you did with me
What must I do and what must I prove
to get you back
here with me
where you belong,

where we belong?
Do you want me to plead? I'm pleading
Do you want me to beg? I'm begging
Do you want me on my knees? I'm kneeling
just say it, state it, record it, videotape it, notarize it
whatever, whenever, wherever, however
I'll do it
whoever, whatsonever
I'll no longer screw it
you must never, ever
share your evening laughter
and morning after glow
with him
let's not make this December
eternally remembered
by your love's removal
and your final disapproval
of me
mi nuh know wha mi a go do if you nuh deh ya wit me
I guess I should have known from all the befores
that when it's all said and done
I don't want to be
I won't stand to be
I refuse to be
anything but YOURS
so don't think you're going to touch me in the morning and then just walk
away
'cause this aint no Motown melody
and this is not the same ole song
and these are not the tears of a clown
and this is no good morning heartache
just a ball of confusion
and a quiet storm
that's easy like Sunday morning

'cause you're 3 times a lady
and I never can say goodbye
to you

How could you?

Subtle clues
often ignored
this time is different
wasn't your usual snore

calling out an unfamiliar name
turning away from my embrace
getting up to answer your cell
never once looking me in the face

your girlfriend is not feeling well
you say in a whisper
you go to the other room
your voice now so crisper

you come back to bed
and I beckon you to hold
but you refuse my affection
stating you are nursing a cold

something is amiss
something is awry
I'll get to the bottom of this
as I peck you goodbye

checked for you at work
to see how your day is going
your Admin says you're out sick today
and is surprised that I'm not knowing

we get together for dinner
and not a word is said

about you not being at work
as you slice and butter your bread

you go on and on
about how your day went
a board meeting, an analyst review
and I'm noticing a new scent

game recognizes game
a player recognizes a player
a preacher recognizes a pimp
and I recognize that I'm going to have slay her

Does she really think it's this easy?
Does she really think I'm that shot out?
Does she really think her pussy's that good?
Does she really think I wouldn't find out?

I lay in the cut
Academy Award performances I give
And this witch don't even know
She's got less than 48 hours to live

now I'm Dr. Jekyl and Mr. Hyde
Two Face and Freddy Krueger
I slow wine her and slow dine her
with Stolichnaya and fresh beluga

on to the dance floor
to perform a Beyonce Bounce
then back to our table
where I have something to announce

I saw you with him
then I had you followed

not so proper and prim
as the tape shows, you swallowed

and you giving a massage
in the middle of the garage
and you in a ménage
me hoping it's a mirage

didn't know you could get down like that
taking backshots and snapshots
and whipping it around like that

didn't know you could get up like that
a triple Lutz-double toe loop combination
with the judges giving you 10's because you are all that

didn't know you could get over like that
accepting a medallion for riding his stallion
and working it out like that

didn't know you could get under like that
no gagging, no choking, all bragging, deep stroking
and taking it all like that

so it all boils down to this, huh?
was I really getting on your nerves?
did you no longer want to be disturbed?
I thought I gave you all that you wanted
but your departure is leaving me oh so haunted
cause there is just no reasonable explanation
for your sudden transformation
and postcards of scenic destinations
that I was not part of the vacation's equation

you're laughing, huh, do you think this is funny?
are you leaving me cause he can give you more money?
are you leaving me cause he can give you more lovin?
is there still a lil bun in your hoppin, poppin oven?

and how am I supposed to be sure
that this bundle of joy is not mine
and how am I supposed to be certain
you weren't faking those orgasms all the time
and how am I supposed to be convinced
that you meant what you said and you meant what you did
and how am I supposed to be assured
that you were with your girls when you were sun bathing in Madrid
and how am I supposed to be confident
that when you signed, "Siempre contigo"
you weren't with him in the bay of Montego

everybody plays the fool sometimes
I thought I was your Ace of Spades
your King of Hearts
I treated you like the Queen of Diamonds
but you Jacked me with your Clubs
and now I'm feeling like a big dummy
when I thought we were partners in the game of love and at playing gin
rummy

if you're gonna walk on my heart, then at least take your damn shoes off
and if you're gonna walk on my heart, then at least wipe your damn feet off
and if you're gonna walk on my heart, then at least...oh why the fuck am I
stressing?
I just want to know how in the hell are you gonna cheat on me *AND* your hus-
band???

A Mother's Lament

I did it.
Yes, I admit it.
I've fucked up again and for the umpteenth time.
You just need to move on and let me be
Mama, don't you hear me? Just let me be!
I'm too busy trying to release cranial endorphins through
cheap vodka,
laced weed,
pumping joy and pain into my veins,
sucking on glass dicks,
drinking cough syrup,
inhaling white substances of any kind…
anything so that I can simply feel ALIVE!
You don't understand.
It's hard out here for a Black Man.
I've got degrees from here and there
yet they don't want to give me nothing.
I'm tired of kissing whitey's ass
and
not getting my just due.
Where's my 40 acres and a mule?

With tears powerful enough to melt Antartic glaciers,
she allows them to form and release.
She inhales deeply, holds it and slowly exhales.
She looks up to the heavens,
closes her eyes tightly for a few seconds,
opens them and liberates a blood-curdling scream,
"Get your black ass up right now!
You are getting the fuck out of here
and
going into rehab,

the unemployment office,
the welfare office,
to church
or a mosque
or anywhere else you think may be necessary
to provide you with the much needed assistance that you require.
but you will no longer sit on your ass as I get up to go to work each and
every damn day!
I brought you into this world
and I'll take you out of it!
you will no longer dishonor your father's memory!
you will no longer disgrace me in front of my neighbors and church folk!
you will no longer bring shame to this family's name!
you will get up and leave and come back employed!
I do not care if it is bagging groceries at Pathmark
or shining shoes at Penn Station
or picking up waste for the trash station
you will leave this house today and come back with a job, dammit
now look what you made me do
you done gone and made me act like my Mama
and you know that bitch was crazy
but I'm gonna have to save you from yourself
or deliver you to your maker
it's up to you
now what's it gonna be?
Are you gonna be a man?
Are you gonna take responsibility for your inactivity?
Are you gonna…?

"Damn, Mama, why it gotta be all dat? Alright, already, I'm getting my ass
up and outta your house."

"Star Jones, please give me the strength to refrain from going upside his head with my new Payless Pump! Come here and give me a kiss! Here's $20. Now you promise you gonna find something today? You promise?"

Looking around the room for his favorite crack pipe, "Yes, Mama, I promise."

For Miss Rosa

She simply said "NO"
wasn't loud about it
didn't have to shout about it
didn't get all ignorant about it
she simply said "NO"
I will not get up
I will not move to the back of the bus
and a revolution was born
what joy it was to see and listen to her in 1995 at the Million Man March.
Upon her introduction, there was a thunderous roar of approval and affection from the multitudes and multitudes of Men that to this day, when recalling the memory, sends chills through my body

It was the ultimate acknowledgement that this woman, this Black woman, dared to do what we men, at one time or another, were/are afraid to do…simply say NO.

How it pained me to my DNA sequence when I heard on the news that her home was broken into and that she was attacked by a man, a Black Man.

If my eyes possessed the power to eject deathly laser beam particles, he would have been disintergrated in an instant.

Did he not know?

How could he not know?

Maya Angelou said of her, "Mrs. Parks is for me probably what the Statue of Liberty was for immigrants. She stood for the future, and the better future."

Thank you for teaching future generations about the power of simply saying NO!

Rest now, Mother of the March
Rest now, Mother of the Movement
Rest now, Mother of the Revolution!

All I Ever Wanted...

Me: "Bring your azz over here and suck this dick!"

She: "Why don't you try giving me a little less lovin and a little more truth!"

Me: "You want the truth? You can't handle the truth!"

See, we got these twins
that constantly cry
and need formula
and clothes
and hugs
and attention
and trips to the emergency room
and medicine for colic
and machines for breathing
and then...
you didn't want to give me no more lovin
and you didn't have no food ready for me when I got in from work
and you didn't fix yourself up no more
and you didn't never wanna go nowhere with me
and you just wanted to wallow in your misery
and me...
I was getting claustrophobic living in that studio apartment
and I realized that I wouldn't ever make enough to support the needs of
this family
and I apologize for screwing your crack head sister, Wanda
and I didn't mean for the gun to go off and shoot that lil ole lady behind
the counter
and now...
look at me on my knees
persuasively pleading
hoping for a handout

crying for compassion
praying for a pardon
looking for leniency
a madman seeking mercy
damn
all I ever wanted on that first date was for you to give me a blow job!
How in da fuck did I end up married with kids and here on death row?
Life's a bitch, and then you die!

The Love We Had Stays On My Mind

"Who loves you?"

"You do."

"That's right, and who loves me?"

"I do."

"and you know that. I'll talk to you later, Big Bro…"

And so went our monthly phone call ending ritual
but it wasn't always like this
as there was a time when we didn't acknowledge each other so affectionately

After being missing in action for about 7 years, I paid Peoplefind.com
$39.95 to track him down and once found, and after all these years, we
have finally reconciled our differences and accepted our similarities:

WE, both rancorous and cantankerous

ME, the jealous one because it seemed that **HE** had everything **I** wanted—
being the first born, Mama's love, light skin, *good hair*, the Mr. Olympian
physique, the wife, the kids…

HIM, the jealous one because it seemed that **I** had everything **HE**
wanted—being the youngest, Daddy's love, dark skin, book smarts, a col-
lege education, real estate properties and happily single…

or so he thought

and now every second of every minute of every hour of every day
I'm missing him

Watching Sommore on BET's Classic Comic View causes a volcanic erup-
tion of laughter, and I immediately reach out to speed dial him before real-
izing he is no longer there to pick up any ring tone of mine.

For a while I would call just to hear his voice on the answering machine, that is until Verizon terminated the service and it was just another reminder that he is no longer on this plane of existence for me to talk to.

or so I thought

When I hear OUR song by The Dells, I sing it out loud and hearty knowing full well that his Angel brethren have dropped their harps and encased their ears because my attempted B sharp has fallen far from the pitch it is supposed to be. But I hear him shouting, "Sing it, Walee, sing that song, Lil Bro! Whew, you are doing it to death! Sign him up, Simon, 'cause he's your next American idol!"

I sigh aloud, "...doing it to death." He's so ole school, my Big Bro.
and then a tear starts to form
and I don't attempt to resist the aqua escape
I just let it flow
and then I let them flow
and a teary tidal wave begins accompanied not by any grunts or sighs or wails
for there's no need for any of the dramatics
just a steady downpour and acknowledgement that my emotional levee has been corrupted.

and this just doesn't happen when I'm alone in my thoughts of him
as a seemingly unimportant scene in a movie or
an Alvin Ailey dancer's demi-plié or
a barber's analysis of the community's re-gentrification or
a Terrell Owen's touchdown antic
is all that it takes and there I go
acting out like I'm the only one who has suffered such a loss, who has grieved so much, who at last had admitted that I love and miss my Big Bro so much.

Who knew that when we exchanged that last phone call where we poured our hearts outs and apologized for all the childhood pranks and the adulthood cranks that it would indeed be the last time we communicated:

ME—I'm sorry for replacing the last of the Domino sugar box with Diamond Crystal salt and laughing hysterically as you poured it unto your bowl of cornflakes and later threw up the bitter tasting cereal…

YOU—I'm sorry for PROVING to your prom date that size DOES really matter…

ME—I'm sorry for calling you a white-skinned mama's boy bitch…

YOU—I'm sorry for calling you a nappyheadedtarbabyniggawhoseneed-fordicksurgicalenhancementisonlyoutweighedbyyour needtogrowsomeballssostopalwayswhininglikesomelilbitch…

You just had to go there, didn't you?

And then we laughed and laughed and laughed and laughed. It felt so good, it hurt so good, and we laughed some more comforted that our deceased parents were now smiling down upon us embraced in the knowledge that we have finally made peace with each other, that we had cleared the mark of Cain.

Then you go and have a heart attack while working out at the gym. Not my Big Bro, not Mr. Universe, not Mr. Non-pork eating, not Mr. I run 60 miles a week, not Mr. Non-cigarette smoking, not Mr. Sexual stamina for hours Mandigo warrior…not my Big Bro!

No way can this be true, we just got back together! Lord, how could you do this to me? Not now, Lord, please, not today Lord, not on my birthday, Lord, there's so much more that I have to tell him, Lord, there's so much that he needs to know, Lord, there's so much more that he needs to do, Lord, there's just so much more that I…that he…that we…

Life is just so damn unpredictable.

I know that I'll eventually be able to successfully navigate this emotional roller coaster without wilding out and crying out and breaking down and feeling sorry for myself, but I want him, no, I **NEED** my Big Bro to know that

I'm missing him

and now every second of every minute of every hour of every day
I'm missing him

'cause I need to ask the question, "Who loves me?"
and I need to hear his answer, "I do!"
and I need for him to know that
with my most imperfect pitch but with my most heartfelt affection
I sing in tribute that
the love we had stays on my mind
yes, Big Bro, the love we had stays on my mind…

Chapter 4

The After Dinner Drinks

These literary cocktails were designed to be the perfect end to a wonderful meal. There are two main types of after dinner drinks, digestifs and the creamy sweet kind. Digestifs, such as brandy, port or whiskey help relax the stomach after a meal. Others, like an ass popper, oops, I mean Grasshopper, are simply a sweet, fun dessert. Bottoms up!

I've loved you for a long time
> You do know I'm talking about you. Don't you?

Time Well Spent
> Y'all come back 'round here again now, ya hear?

I've loved you for a long time

I don't get to see you often enough nor as much as I secretly desire. When I do, the communication exchange is mostly a quick "Hello," "How are you today?" and an occasional "How's things with the book?" If you really want to know the truth about it, when I do see you, I force down a raging hard on and use every inner stomach muscle to control the urge to grab you, hold you and force my tongue down your throat. Oh how I wish to taste your cavity and tickle your tonsil and drop to my knees and inhale your scent. But I play it cool, act like all is good and respect the institution of marriage that you are committed to. I offer a friendly, smiling "What's happening with you" and "Good to see you" while lusting that you'll say something with deeper meaning, offer a comparable look of wanting or a smile that says more behind it. But alas, none of the aforementioned are offered. So I attempt to contain the erections and explain away the unrequited affection. When you read this, I hope there is a sense of familiarity. Maybe, just maybe, you'll give me a knowing wink that says while the two of us could never be, you are complimented at the thought. I ask that you forgive my future intense stares from a far. It's just that I'll be looking for a signal that says, "Hey, Walee, what are you doing later...."

Time Well Spent

after all the pages have been turned
and after all the lessons have been learned
maybe now you'll understand me a little bit more
and maybe now you'll understand if I come knocking at your door
naked and with arms outstretched wide
unashamed and uninhibited with nothing to hide
hoping to give your body a helluva ride
but more importantly, to your heart, I want to confide

the lyrics on the preceding pages have been washed, simmered and basted
and I hope your journey with me has been time well wasted
as it has been my pleasure being your chef, waiter and cashier this evening
I hope that **What's On The Menu** was cooked with all the right season-
ings

I trust you have enjoyed the savory sensations and literary creations
and that you go forth and tell a friend
and if you haven't already purchased **Confession is Good for the Soul**
then do so, e-mail me, and we can do this all again

So readily yours,
So incredibly yours,
So edibly yours,

Mmm, mmm good

Affectionately yours,
Confectionally yours,
Erectionally yours,

Love, Walee

Now that you've enjoyed the warm content feeling that comes from an exceptional meal enjoyed to the fullest, sit back and partake in casual conversation with me via _walee@att.net_.

In particular, I'm most interested in which entrée was your favorite and why. Did I hit close to home? Do you know the person(s) I'm referring to? Was there something you absolutely did not like the taste of? These and more of my questions can be responded to so just hit me up.

I thank you for your attention and ask…no, plead…actually beg that you tell a co-worker, family member, friend, hell, even an enemy to run out and order <u>What's on the Menu?</u> by this one-named lyricist called Walee.

I am available for book club discussions, in-store appearances, songwriting publishing negotiations, etc.

Ooh, I just came up with something new…Up, Up and Away…yeah, it's sophomoric but heck, it's the last page and…

From dolls that get blown up

to legs that get thrown up

to boots that get knocked up

to bedframes that get banged up

to asses that get backed up

to pussies that get ate up

to mouths that get filled up

to jokes that get cracked up

to attitudes that get fed up

to noses that get busted up

to relationships that get broke up

to misunderstandings that get cleared up

Ok, I'm gonna stop now as somebody's knocking on my door…

978-0-595-39041-0
0-595-39041-2